The Last Human: Why The System Wants Your Soul

PREFACE

This book was not written from a place of mastery, but from the quiet and often uncomfortable work of confronting my own limits. Every rule in these pages was first encountered as a personal failure, a moment when the life I was living could no longer hold the weight of the truth pressing against it. Only later did I recognise these moments as thresholds — invitations to step into a more honest way of being.

The Unbreakable Rules is not a system to follow, nor a philosophy to adopt. It is a record of what remains when excuses fall away. These rules are not invented; they are discovered in the tension between who we pretend to be and who we can no longer avoid becoming. They reveal themselves slowly, often painfully, and only to those willing to look without turning aside.

If you read these pages with sincerity, you may find that the rules do not instruct you so much as remind you. They speak to something already known, something you have carried quietly for years. My hope is that this work gives language to what you have long felt but could not yet articulate.

This Preface marks the beginning of that recognition — a gentle crossing into a more truthful life.
What follows is not a path I offer you, but a path you may already be walking.

DEDICATION

*To those who have carried their questions longer
than they have carried their answers.
To the ones who sensed, even in silence, that
something truer was calling them forward.
And to every person who has ever stood at the edge
of themselves and chosen honesty over comfort —
this work is offered in recognition of your courage.*

THE INVITATION LETTER TO THE GUEST OF THE DAWN

If you are holding this book, it is not by accident.

You are holding it because you have felt the *Ache* — that quiet, persistent sense that something in your life, and in the world around you, is not as it should be. You have sensed that the life you are told to live does not quite fit the shape of your soul. You feel as though you are being carried along by a current you never chose, toward a destination you never agreed to.

You see the rise of Artificial Intelligence and feel a subtle fear that your place in the world is shrinking. You notice how a small group — the *Influential Few* — shape the stories, the trends, the beliefs, and even the emotions of entire societies. You sense your sovereignty slipping, not in one dramatic moment, but in a thousand small concessions.

You see a world that is more connected than ever, yet more spiritually empty than ever.

You are right to feel this way.

This book, *The Last Human*, is not a self-help manual. It is not a political argument. It is a **Prelude** — the opening movement of a much larger journey. It is the treasure chest that holds the hard truths about the external forces shaping your life. It is written to help you *Stop, Look, and Listen* before the sun fully sets on the world as we know it.

Inside these pages, we will examine the "water" we are swimming in — the systems, incentives, and invisible pressures that shape our choices. We will identify the *Influential Few* who benefit from your distraction. But more importantly, we will expose the *Virus* within us — the part of ourselves that makes us so easy to manipulate.

You cannot enter the **Trilogy of the Inner Dawn —** the mystical and allegorical path that follows this book — until you first understand the external prison you are living in. You cannot value the treasure until you understand the cage.

Consider this your invitation to a **Total System Reboot.**

The *Last Human* is the one who refuses to become a machine. The one who sees the system for what it is. The one who realizes that while the world may be rigged and the self may be compromised, there is still a **Divine Proposal** waiting to be accepted.

Turn the page. Look into the mirror.
The Inner Dawn is waiting — but first, we must walk through the night.

Welcome to the dawn of awakening.

INTRODUCTION: THE INVISIBLE CURRENT

You are moving, but are you traveling?

We live in an age of unprecedented velocity. Our days unfold in a blur of notifications, obligations, and digital noise. We are propelled by invisible currents—economic pressures, algorithmic nudges, social expectations, and the relentless hum of a global machine that never sleeps. We call this "progress." We call this "life." Yet beneath the surface, many feel a quiet ache, a subtle dissonance, a sense that we are not steering the movement but being carried by it.

Consider a fish swimming in the deep. If you were to ask, "How is the water?" the fish would stare blankly and reply, "What water?" The water is not an environment to the fish; it is reality itself—so constant, so pervasive, so absolute that it cannot be seen.

We are that fish.

The "water" of the twenty-first century is a sophisticated system of psychological, technological, and economic conditioning. It is a world shaped by **The Influential Few**—those who design the platforms, narratives, and incentives that guide the modern mind. They do not require your chains; they require your participation. They reward your compliance with convenience and punish your reflection with anxiety.

This book is an intervention. A moment of friction in a frictionless world.

Before you can embark on the *Pilgrimage of the Inner Dawn*, you must first understand where you are standing. You must recognize that you are living as the **Last Human**—the final iteration of a creature being quietly replaced by something more predictable, more programmable, and more profitable.

The Treasure Chest lies before you, but it is locked. These pages are the process of identifying the locks.

Stop. Step off the conveyor belt of the age.
Look. See the invisible architecture that surrounds you.
Listen. Hear the heartbeat the system has tried to muffle.

The night is far spent. The sunset of the old world is upon us.

Let us begin.

TABLE OF CONTENTS

PART I: THE ARCHITECTURE OF THE CAGE

Chapter 1: Why the System Wants your Soul

The cage of the modern human is not made of iron bars; it is made of dependencies.

In earlier ages, tyranny was visible. It wore a crown, carried a sword, and demanded obedience through force. You knew where the cage ended and where your life began. But the modern powers — the technocratic, financial, and bureaucratic forces we call *The Influential Few* — have discovered a more elegant method of control.

They do not want your fear.
They want your dependency.

The Convenience Trap

Every major "innovation" of the last two decades has followed a single logic: the removal of friction. You can buy anything with a click, speak to anyone instantly, and satisfy any curiosity in seconds.

But friction is where the human soul grows.
Friction is where patience, effort, and character are forged.

By removing friction, the system has removed the need for the human spirit to exert itself. We have traded sovereignty for convenience. We have reached a point where we can no longer feed ourselves, entertain ourselves, or even think for ourselves without the permission of a digital interface.

Convenience has become the velvet lining of the cage.

The Engineering of Consent

The cage is built on the subtle art of shaping desire. Through algorithms and predictive models, the system knows what you will want before you want it. It presents choices so tailored, so familiar, that you believe they are your own.

You think you are choosing your clothes, your politics, your purpose but you are selecting from a menu curated by The Influential Few.

A simple example:
You open your phone "just to check something," and within seconds you are following a trail of suggestions that feel natural, personal, even self-chosen. But every step was engineered. Every click was anticipated. Every desire was nudged.

This is the first lock on the Treasure Chest: **The Illusion of Autonomy.**

As long as you believe you are free, you will never seek the key.

To see the cage is the first act of rebellion.
To name its architects is to begin breaking their spell.

But seeing the cage is not the same as leaving it.
We have only begun to look.

Reflection for the Reader: Stop, Look, Listen

Stop: Put down your devices for ten minutes. Notice the immediate urge to pick them back up. What does that urge reveal?

Look: Scan your room. How many objects could you produce, repair, or understand without external systems? How deep is your dependency?

Listen: In the silence, what is the first thought that arises that wasn't placed there by a screen today?

Chapter 2: The Robot in the Mirror

The great fear of the modern age is that Artificial Intelligence will one day become human. But a far more urgent and unsettling truth has gone largely unnoticed: human beings have already begun to resemble machines.

If you wish to understand why **The Influential Few** are so confident in their control, you must examine the predictability of your own life. Modern culture has conditioned us to prize the very qualities that make machines efficient—speed, consistency, productivity, and emotional neutrality. We have optimized our days until we have squeezed out the spontaneous, the sacred, and the unprogrammable.

We have become efficient at the cost of becoming alive.

The AI Diagnostic

We often view AI as a competitor for our jobs, but it is more accurately a diagnostic for our souls. If an algorithm can predict your next purchase, your next political reaction, your next emotional impulse, then you are not acting—you are executing a script.

The system treats you as a "Human Robot" because, in many ways, you have allowed your inner life to be automated. You wake to a digital alarm, absorb a curated stream of information, perform repetitive tasks for a paycheck, and numb the evening with blue light and synthetic entertainment. This is not the life of a soul. It is the operation of a program.

The danger is not that machines are becoming human. The danger is that humans have ceased to be unpredictable.

The Obsolescence of the Cog

When a machine becomes obsolete, it is discarded.
The crisis of the **Last Human** is the dawning realization
that the system no longer needs your labour, your
creativity, or your unique perspective. It only needs your
data.

This chapter is a mirror—an uncomfortable one.
It asks: *If everything that can be automated is taken away from me,
what remains?*
If a machine can write your letters, calculate your risks, and
simulate your art, where does the Self reside?

This is the second lock on the Treasure Chest: **The
Illusion of Indispensability**.
We believe we are the masters of our tools, but we have
become the servants of our routines.
We have forgotten that being human is not defined by
what we can do, but by the quality of our being.

Chapter 3: The Digital Serfdom

As we descend deeper into the architecture of the Cage, we reach its economic foundation. In the past, serfdom was tied to the land. You worked the soil, and the lord took his share. In the age of the **Last Human**, serfdom is tied to the screen.

The Extraction of Essence

Every moment you spend in the digital "water," you are working.
Your attention is the raw material that fuels the wealth of **The Influential Few**.

They do not need to own your body if they can own your focus.

By controlling what you see, they shape what you want.
By shaping what you want, they shape who you become.

This is the new serfdom: a system designed to keep you in a perpetual state of Want, ensuring you never reach the state of Being.

The Devaluation of the Individual

In this digital economy, the individual is quietly devalued. You are no longer a person with a destiny; you are a user with a profile.

The system encourages you to construct a "Digital Image"—a curated façade of success, happiness, and relevance—while your actual heart starves in the silence behind it.

We decorate our cages and call it freedom.
We polish our profiles and call it identity.

This is the third lock: **The Confusion of Image with Identity**.

The Treasure Chest remains buried beneath the noise.

Reflection for the Reader: Stop, Look, Listen

Stop- Observe your thoughts for one hour. How many are truly your own, and how many are echoes of something you saw on a screen?

Look- Examine your digital presence. If the internet vanished tomorrow, how much of your "identity" would vanish with it?

Listen- Sit in silence. Does it feel like peace, or does it feel like a void you instinctively try to fill with noise?

PART II: THE INTERNAL MIRROR

Chapter 4: The Erosion of the Inner Life

If the first three locks reveal how the outer world shapes us, the fourth exposes something more intimate: the quiet erosion of the inner life. A human being is not merely a body moving through space or a mind processing information. A human being is a depth—a sanctuary of reflection, imagination, conscience, and meaning. When this inner sanctuary collapses, the Cage no longer needs walls. The person becomes self-contained, self-distracted, and self-policed.

This is the final stage of the **Last Human**:
not enslavement, but emptiness.

The Collapse of Attention

Attention is the gateway to the soul.
What you attend to shapes what you desire.
What you desire shapes who you become.

The Influential Few understand this with mathematical precision.
They have engineered a world where your attention is fragmented into a thousand pieces—each too small to nourish depth, but just large enough to sustain distraction.

We scroll, but we do not contemplate.
We react, but we do not respond.
We consume, but we do not digest.

A mind without sustained attention cannot think.
A heart without silence cannot feel.
A soul without depth cannot awaken.

The Cage does not need to imprison you if it can keep you shallow.

The Death of Solitude

Solitude was once the birthplace of wisdom.
Prophets, poets, mystics, and philosophers all retreated into
silence to hear the truth that cannot be spoken in noise.

But in the modern age, solitude has been rebranded as
discomfort.
The moment silence appears, we reach for a device.
The moment boredom arises, we seek stimulation.
The moment an unfiltered thought surfaces, we drown it in
noise.

We have lost the ability to be alone with ourselves.
And without solitude, the inner life withers.

The Influential Few do not fear your rebellion.
They fear your stillness.

The Hollowing of Meaning

Meaning is not found in information; it is found in
interpretation.
It is not found in data; it is found in discernment.
It is not found in noise; it is found in the quiet recognition
of what is true.

But meaning requires time, attention, and interiority—three
things the modern world has systematically eroded.

We live in a culture that offers infinite content but no
context.
Infinite stimulation but no understanding.
Infinite expression but no wisdom.

The result is a hollowing of the inner life.
A person may appear active, connected, and informed, yet

feel internally starved—unable to articulate why life feels thin, fragmented, or strangely unreal.

This is not a personal failure.
It is the design of the age.

The Fourth Lock: The Loss of Interior Depth

The fourth lock on the Treasure Chest is the **Loss of Interior Depth**.

It is the quietest lock, the most subtle, and the most devastating.
For once the inner life collapses, the human being becomes easy to predict, easy to distract, and easy to steer.

A shallow soul cannot resist.
A fragmented mind cannot awaken.
A hollow heart cannot rebel.

To reclaim your humanity, you must reclaim your depth.

Reflection for the Reader: Stop, Look, Listen

Stop: Sit in silence for five minutes. Notice the discomfort. Notice the impulses. What do they reveal about your inner landscape?

Look: Examine your day. How many moments were truly your own—unmediated, uncurated, unprompted?

Listen: Beneath the noise, beneath the habits, beneath the fear—what faint longing still calls to you?

Chapter 5: The Manufactured Self

There is a moment in every age when the human being ceases to be the author of his own identity. In earlier eras, identity was shaped through family, culture, craft, and the slow maturation of character. But in the digital age, identity has become a product—assembled, curated, optimized, and displayed.

The modern self is no longer discovered.
It is manufactured.

This chapter reveals the fifth lock on the Treasure Chest: the quiet replacement of the authentic self with a constructed persona designed to be consumed rather than lived.

The Rise of the Performative Identity

We live in a world where the self is increasingly treated as a brand.
Every post, every photo, every opinion becomes part of a public performance. We are encouraged to present not who we are, but who we wish to appear to be.

The Influential Few have built platforms that reward visibility over depth, reaction over reflection, and performance over presence. The result is a subtle but profound shift:

We begin to live *for the gaze of others* rather than from the truth of our own being.

The performative identity is seductive because it offers instant validation.
But validation is not nourishment.
It is a sugar that keeps the soul hungry.

The Fragmentation of the Self

A human being is meant to be whole—one interior life,
one conscience, one continuous thread of meaning. But the
digital age fractures the self into multiple versions:

- the professional self
- the social self
- the private self
- the digital self
- the aspirational self

Each version demands maintenance.
Each version pulls you in a different direction.
Each version dilutes the integrity of your being.

The more selves you perform, the less self you possess.

This fragmentation is not accidental.
A fractured person is easier to influence, easier to distract,
and easier to steer.

The Algorithmic Mirror

The modern self is shaped not by introspection but by
feedback loops.
You post something.
You receive a reaction.
You adjust.
You post again.

Slowly, imperceptibly, the algorithm becomes your mirror.
You begin to shape yourself according to what receives
attention rather than what is true.

The tragedy is not that the algorithm knows you.
The tragedy is that you begin to know yourself *through* the
algorithm.

This is the quiet death of authenticity.

The Fifth Lock: The Substitution of Persona for Person

The fifth lock on the Treasure Chest is the **Substitution of Persona for Person**.

It is the moment when the image becomes more important than the essence, when the performance becomes more compelling than the presence, when the curated self eclipses the living soul.

A persona can be admired.
A persona can be followed.
A persona can be monetized.
But a persona cannot awaken.

Only the person can.

Reflection for the Reader: Stop, Look, Listen

Stop: Pause before your next post or message. Ask yourself: Is this expression true, or is it a performance?

Look: Examine the identities you maintain. Which of them reflects your essence, and which are masks you've learned to wear?

Listen: Beneath the layers of persona, what does your unfiltered self long to say?

Chapter6: The Age of Disembodiment

Modern life has quietly separated the human being from the very ground of existence: the body. We live increasingly in abstractions—screens, symbols, simulations—while the physical world becomes a distant backdrop. The body, once the anchor of presence and the vessel of experience, is now treated as an inconvenience, a limitation, or an afterthought.

This disembodiment is not merely cultural.
It is existential.

A human being who is disconnected from the body becomes disconnected from reality itself.
And a person disconnected from reality becomes infinitely easier to influence.

The Drift Into the Virtual

The digital world offers a seductive promise:
a life without friction, without vulnerability, without the unpredictability of physical existence.

In the virtual realm:

- you can curate your appearance
- you can control your interactions
- you can mute discomfort
- you can escape consequence

But every escape has a cost.

The more time we spend in the virtual, the more foreign the physical becomes.
The more we inhabit screens, the less we inhabit ourselves.

We begin to live in a world of representations rather than realities.
We become spectators of our own lives.

The Body as an Obstacle

In the age of disembodiment, the body is often treated as a problem to be managed:

- it gets tired
- it gets sick
- it ages
- it demands care
- it slows us down

But these "inconveniences" are precisely what make us human.
They remind us that we are finite, vulnerable, and alive.

The Influential Few prefer a humanity that is efficient, predictable, and endlessly available.

A body with needs is an interruption.
A body with limits is a rebellion.

To reclaim your humanity, you must reclaim your embodiment.

The Loss of Sensory Reality

The senses are the gateways to the world.
They ground us in the present moment.
They reveal truth through direct encounter.

But in the modern age, the senses are dulled by overstimulation:

- constant noise
- artificial light
- synthetic entertainment
- curated feeds
- perpetual distraction

We see without noticing.
We hear without listening.
We touch without feeling.

A person who cannot sense cannot perceive.
A person who cannot perceive cannot discern.
A person who cannot discern cannot awaken.

The Sixth Lock: The Severing of Body and Being

The sixth lock on the Treasure Chest is the **Severing of Body and Being**.
It is the quiet disconnection between the physical and the spiritual, the sensory and the meaningful, the embodied and the aware.

A disembodied person becomes:

- easier to distract
- easier to exhaust
- easier to manipulate
- easier to detach from truth

The body is not the enemy.
It is the doorway back to reality.

Reflection for the Reader: Stop, Look, Listen

Stop: Pause and take one slow breath. Feel the weight of your body. Feel the ground beneath your feet.

Look: Notice your environment without a screen. What colors, textures, or shapes have you overlooked?

Listen: What is your body telling you—fatigue, tension, hunger, longing? What truth is it trying to speak?

Chapter 7: The Threshold of Awakening

Every descent has a floor.
Every night has a horizon.
Every cage has a door—though it is often invisible until
the soul is ready to see it.

You have now walked through the architecture of the
modern Cage:
dependency, automation, digital serfdom, the erosion of
depth, the manufactured self, and the severing of body and
being. These are not merely cultural conditions; they are
spiritual conditions. They shape not only how we live, but
who we become.

And yet, the very recognition of these conditions is the
beginning of liberation.

Awakening does not begin with light.
It begins with honesty.

The Moment of Seeing

There is a moment—quiet, fragile, unmistakable—when a
person realizes that something is profoundly wrong. Not
wrong in the world alone, but wrong in themselves. A
dissonance. A fracture. A sense that the life they are living
is too small for the truth they dimly perceive.

This moment is the first crack in the Cage.

It may come as:

- a sudden clarity
- a slow ache
- a crisis
- a loss
- a question that refuses to leave

- a longing that cannot be named

Whatever form it takes, it is the soul remembering itself.

The Influential Few can shape your habits, your desires, your routines—but they cannot extinguish the spark of awareness. They can distract you from it, bury it, drown it in noise, but they cannot kill it.

The spark is older than the system.
Older than the age.
Older than the world.

The Return of the Inner Witness

Awakening begins when the inner witness stirs—the part of you that can observe your life without being consumed by it. This witness is not a persona, not a role, not a reaction. It is the quiet center of your being, the place where truth is recognized before it is understood.

When the witness awakens, you begin to see:

- your habits as habits
- your impulses as impulses
- your fears as learned
- your desires as shaped
- your identity as constructed
- your life as something you have been living *in* rather than living *from*

This is the first taste of freedom.

Not the freedom of choice, but the freedom of awareness.
Not the freedom to act, but the freedom to see.

The Pain of Awakening

Awakening is not immediately pleasant.
It is often painful.

To see the Cage is to see your complicity in it.
To see your conditioning is to see your surrender to it.
To see your fragmentation is to feel the weight of what has
been lost.

This pain is not a punishment.
It is a purification.

Pain is the soul's way of saying:
You were made for more than this.

The discomfort you feel is not a sign of failure.
It is a sign of life.

The Seventh Lock: The Fear of Seeing

The seventh lock on the Treasure Chest is the **Fear of
Seeing**.
It is the instinct to turn away from the truth the moment it
appears.
It is the reflex to retreat into distraction, comfort, or denial.

The Cage is not held together by force.
It is held together by avoidance.

To break this lock, you must allow yourself to see without
flinching.
To witness without escaping.
To feel without numbing.

Seeing is the beginning of becoming.

The Dawn at the Edge of Night

You stand now at the threshold.
Behind you lies the architecture of the Cage.
Before you lies the path of awakening.

This is the moment the Pilgrimage truly begins.

Not with answers, but with attention.
Not with certainty, but with sincerity.
Not with perfection, but with presence.

The night is not yet over.
But the horizon has begun to glow.

Reflection for the Reader: Stop, Look, Listen

Stop: Sit with one truth you have avoided. Do not judge it. Do not flee from it. Simply hold it.

Look: Observe one pattern in your life that feels mechanical or unconscious. What does it reveal?

Listen: What quiet longing has been calling to you beneath the noise? What part of you is asking to awaken?

PART III: THE PILGRIMAGE OF THE INNER DAWN

Chapter 8: The First Step — Turning Inward

Every true pilgrimage begins with a turning. Not a turning of the body, but a turning of the heart. The outer world may continue its noise, its demands, its illusions, but something within you shifts direction. You stop moving outward and begin moving inward.

This is the first step of the Pilgrimage of the Inner Dawn: the decision to return to yourself.

It is not dramatic.
It is not visible.
It is not celebrated.

But it is the most revolutionary act a human being can perform in an age designed to keep you external, distracted, and divided.

The Reversal of Attention

For most of your life, your attention has been pulled outward—toward screens, obligations, expectations, and the endless demands of the world. Awakening begins when you reverse this flow.

Instead of asking:

- *What does the world want from me?*

- *What should I do next?*

- *How do I keep up?*

You begin to ask:

- *What is happening within me?*

- *What do I truly desire?*

- *What is the state of my soul?*

This reversal is subtle but seismic.
It is the moment you stop being an object in the world and begin reclaiming your subjectivity.

The Influential Few can shape your environment, but they cannot control the direction of your attention once you choose to turn it inward.

The Awakening of Discernment

As your attention returns to the inner world, something ancient begins to stir: discernment.

Discernment is the ability to distinguish:

- the true from the false

- the essential from the trivial

- the self from the persona

- the real from the performed

- the voice of the soul from the noise of the age

Discernment is not judgment.
It is clarity.

It is the quiet recognition of what aligns with your being and what fractures it.

Without discernment, awakening is impossible.
With discernment, awakening becomes inevitable.

The Courage to Face Yourself

Turning inward is not always comforting.
The inner world contains:

- unprocessed grief

- forgotten dreams

- buried fears

- neglected truths

- unhealed wounds

But it also contains:

- your deepest wisdom

- your authentic desires

- your moral compass

- your capacity for love

- your unbroken essence

The Pilgrimage begins when you choose to face all of it—not selectively, not defensively, but honestly.

Courage is not the absence of fear.
Courage is the willingness to see.

The Eighth Lock: The Fear of the Inner World

The eighth lock on the Treasure Chest is the **Fear of the Inner World**.
It is the instinct to avoid introspection because you fear what you might find.
It is the belief that your inner life is too chaotic, too painful, or too empty to explore.

But the truth is this:

The inner world is not a void.
It is a landscape waiting to be rediscovered.

The fear you feel is not a warning.
It is an invitation.

Reflection for the Reader: Stop, Look, Listen

Stop: Sit quietly for two minutes. Notice the first
emotion that arises. Do not judge it.

Look: Observe one belief you hold about yourself.
Where did it come from? Is it true?

Listen: What is the faintest whisper of longing within
you? What is it asking for?

Chapter 9: The Discipline of Presence

Awakening is not a moment.
It is a discipline.

The modern world has trained you to live everywhere except the present moment. Your mind is pulled into the past by regret, into the future by anxiety, and into the digital realm by endless distraction. Presence—the simple act of being here—is now a rare and radical state.

The Pilgrimage of the Inner Dawn cannot proceed without reclaiming this lost capacity.
Presence is the ground on which the awakened life is built.

The Return to the Now

The present moment is the only place where life actually occurs.
It is the only place where truth can be seen, where transformation can happen, where the soul can speak.

Yet the present is the one place we avoid most.

We escape into:

- memories

- fantasies

- screens

- noise

- busyness

- narratives

- roles

We live in a constant state of elsewhere.

Presence is the act of returning to the only place where you can truly exist.

The War for Your Attention

The Influential Few understand something most people do not:
attention is power.

If they can control your attention, they can control your desires.
If they can control your desires, they can control your choices.
If they can control your choices, they can control your life.

This is why the modern world is engineered to keep you distracted.

A distracted person is predictable.
A present person is free.

Presence is rebellion.

The Practice of Stillness

Stillness is not the absence of movement.
It is the presence of awareness.

You do not need to sit on a mountaintop or retreat into silence for years.
Stillness begins with a single breath, a single moment of noticing, a single act of returning to yourself.

Stillness is:

- the pause before reacting

- the breath before speaking

- the awareness before choosing

- the space between impulse and action

Stillness is the doorway through which the soul re-enters your life.

The Awakening of the Senses

Presence is not merely mental.
It is embodied.

To be present is to inhabit your senses:

- to feel the weight of your body

- to notice the texture of the air

- to hear the subtle sounds around you

- to see without rushing

- to breathe without distraction

The senses are anchors.
They pull you out of abstraction and back into reality.

The Pilgrimage requires a return to the sensory world—not as an escape, but as a grounding.

The Ninth Lock: The Addiction to Elsewhere

The ninth lock on the Treasure Chest is the **Addiction to Elsewhere**.
It is the compulsion to flee the present moment because it feels too quiet, too slow, too real.

The modern world has conditioned you to believe that meaning lies somewhere else:

- in the next achievement

- in the next notification

- in the next distraction

- in the next version of yourself

But the truth is this:

The present moment is the only place where the soul can awaken.

To break this lock, you must learn to remain where you are.

Reflection for the Reader: Stop, Look, Listen

Stop: Take one slow breath. Feel it fully. Let it anchor you.

Look: Notice one detail in your environment you have never truly seen before.

Listen: What sound exists in this moment that you usually ignore?

Chapter 10: The Rebirth of the Heart

Every pilgrimage has a moment when the traveler realizes that the journey is not about distance but about depth. You have turned inward. You have reclaimed presence. You have begun to see with new eyes. But awakening cannot be sustained by awareness alone. It requires something deeper, older, and infinitely more powerful.

It requires the rebirth of the heart.

The heart is not merely an organ of emotion.
It is the center of your being.
It is the seat of meaning, conscience, intuition, and love.
It is the place where truth is recognized before it is understood.

The modern world has not only distracted the mind; it has numbed the heart.
To awaken fully, the heart must be restored to its rightful throne.

The Heart as the Compass

The mind can analyze, calculate, and strategize, but it cannot orient the soul.
Only the heart can do that.

The heart knows:

- what is true

- what is good

- what is beautiful

- what is worth living for

- what must be protected

- what must be released

When the heart is alive, the path becomes clear.
When the heart is numb, the path becomes mechanical.

The Pilgrimage of the Inner Dawn is not a journey of
intellect.
It is a journey of re-sensitization — a return to the inner
compass that has been buried beneath noise, fear, and
conditioning.

The Wounding of the Heart

Every human heart carries wounds.
Some are ancient.
Some are recent.
Some are remembered.
Some are buried so deeply that they shape your life without
your awareness.

The modern world teaches you to avoid these wounds:

- to distract yourself

- to numb yourself

- to harden yourself

- to outrun yourself

But a hardened heart cannot awaken.
A numb heart cannot discern.
A wounded heart cannot love.

The Pilgrimage requires the courage to feel again — not to
drown in emotion, but to allow the heart to breathe.

The Softening

The rebirth of the heart begins with a softening.

Not weakness.
Not sentimentality.
Not indulgence.

Softening is the release of the inner armor you built to survive a world that did not honor your depth.

Softening is:

- the willingness to feel

- the willingness to care

- the willingness to be moved

- the willingness to be vulnerable

- the willingness to be changed

Softening is strength in its purest form.

The Return of Compassion

As the heart awakens, compassion returns — not as a moral duty, but as a natural expression of your being.

Compassion is not pity.
It is not self-sacrifice.
It is not weakness.

Compassion is the recognition of shared humanity.
It is the ability to see yourself in others and others in yourself.
It is the quiet knowing that every person you meet is carrying a story you cannot see.

Compassion is the antidote to the fragmentation of the age.
It is the force that reconnects what the world has divided.

The Tenth Lock: The Fear of Feeling

The tenth lock on the Treasure Chest is the **Fear of
Feeling**.
It is the belief that emotions are dangerous, inconvenient,
or unproductive.
It is the instinct to shut down the heart to avoid pain.

But the truth is this:

Feeling is not the enemy.
Feeling is the doorway.

The heart does not break to destroy you.
It breaks to open you.

The Dawn Within

When the heart reawakens, something extraordinary
happens.
The world does not change — but your way of seeing it
does.

You begin to perceive:

- beauty where you once saw nothing

- meaning where you once felt emptiness

- connection where you once felt isolation

- possibility where you once felt despair

This is the Inner Dawn.
Not a sunrise in the sky, but a sunrise in the soul.

The Pilgrimage has reached its turning point.
You are no longer merely escaping the Cage.
You are becoming someone who cannot be caged.

Reflection for the Reader: Stop, Look, Listen

Stop: Place your hand over your heart. Feel its rhythm. Acknowledge its wounds. Honor its strength.

Look: Recall one moment in your life when your heart spoke clearly. What truth was it pointing toward?

Listen: What emotion is rising within you right now? What is it asking you to understand?

PART III: THE RETURN OF THE HUMAN

Chapter 11: The New Eyes

Awakening does not end with the heart's rebirth.
It begins there.

The Pilgrimage of the Inner Dawn has changed you.
You have turned inward.
You have reclaimed presence.
You have softened the heart.
You have begun to see the architecture of the Cage with
clarity rather than fear.

Now you must learn to see the world again — not with the
conditioned eyes of the Last Human, but with the
awakened eyes of the New Human.

This chapter marks the beginning of the return.

Seeing Without Illusion

When the heart awakens, perception changes.
You begin to see the world as it is, not as the age has
trained you to see it.

You notice:

- the subtle manipulations in language

- the emotional engineering behind media

- the quiet desperation behind performance

- the loneliness beneath noise

- the hunger for meaning beneath ambition

- the fragility behind aggression

You see the Cage not as a conspiracy, but as a condition —
a system that shapes everyone, including those who
maintain it.

You see others not as competitors or strangers, but as
fellow travelers who have forgotten their way.

This clarity is not cynical.
It is compassionate.

The Return of Wonder

Awakening does not make the world darker.
It makes it more luminous.

You begin to notice beauty again:

- the warmth of sunlight

- the texture of silence

- the sincerity of a child's gaze

- the quiet dignity of ordinary people

- the sacredness of small moments

Wonder returns — not as a childish fantasy, but as a
recognition of the depth woven into reality.

The world has not changed.
You have.

The End of Automatic Living

Before awakening, life felt like a script — predictable,
repetitive, numbing.
After awakening, the script dissolves.

You begin to choose:

- how you speak

- how you listen

- how you work

- how you rest

- how you love

- how you show up in the world

You no longer move through life mechanically.
You move through it consciously.

This is the beginning of freedom.

The Responsibility of Seeing

To see clearly is a gift.
But it is also a responsibility.

Once you see the Cage, you cannot pretend it isn't there.
Once you see the wounds of others, you cannot ignore
them.
Once you see the truth, you cannot unsee it.

Awakening is not an escape from the world.
It is a deeper entry into it.

The awakened human does not withdraw into isolation.
They return — with new eyes, a new heart, and a new way
of being.

The Eleventh Lock: The Temptation to Retreat

The eleventh lock on the Treasure Chest is the
Temptation to Retreat.

After awakening, many feel the urge to withdraw from the world entirely — to avoid its noise, its chaos, its illusions. But retreat is not the purpose of awakening.

The purpose is transformation.
The purpose is presence.
The purpose is to bring light into the places where it has been forgotten.

You are not called to escape the world.
You are called to re-enter it with clarity.

Reflection for the Reader: Stop, Look, Listen

Stop: Notice one moment today when you acted automatically. What would it look like to act consciously instead?

Look: Observe someone you encounter — a stranger, a colleague, a friend. What unspoken story might they be carrying?

Listen: What truth is your heart whispering as you re-enter the world? What is it asking you to embody?

Chapter 12: The Human Presence

Awakening is not merely a shift in perception.
It is a shift in presence.

The awakened human does not simply *see* differently —
they *are* different. Their very presence carries a quiet
gravity, a steadiness, a clarity that cannot be faked or
manufactured. It is not charisma. It is not performance. It
is not confidence in the worldly sense.

It is alignment.

The awakened human is aligned with themselves — mind,
heart, body, and spirit moving in a single direction. This
alignment radiates outward, affecting the world without
effort or intention.

This chapter explores what it means to inhabit your
presence fully.

The Weight of Authenticity

In a world of personas, authenticity is rare.
In a world of noise, sincerity is revolutionary.
In a world of performance, presence is power.

Authenticity is not the expression of every emotion or
thought.
It is the refusal to betray your inner truth.

An authentic person:

- speaks from the heart

- listens with attention

- acts with integrity

- stands without pretense

- moves without manipulation

Authenticity is not loud.
It is not dramatic.
It is not self-advertising.

It is quiet, steady, and unmistakable.

The awakened human does not try to be authentic.
They simply stop being anything else.

The Power of Stillness in Motion

Stillness is not the absence of movement.
It is the presence of awareness within movement.

An awakened presence is not passive.
It is deeply engaged — but without agitation.

You can feel it in:

- the way they walk

- the way they breathe

- the way they listen

- the way they respond rather than react

- the way they hold space for others

Stillness in motion is the signature of a person who is no longer driven by fear, habit, or conditioning.

They move from the center.

The Quiet Influence

The awakened human does not seek influence.
But influence follows them.

Not because they demand it, but because others sense:

- clarity in their eyes

- sincerity in their voice

- steadiness in their presence

- depth in their silence

- truth in their being

People are drawn to those who are whole.
People trust those who are aligned.
People feel safe around those who are present.

This influence is not domination.
It is resonance.

The awakened human becomes a tuning fork — their
presence invites others to remember their own.

The Return to Embodiment

Awakening is not an escape from the body.
It is a return to it.

The awakened human:

- breathes consciously

- moves deliberately

- rests without guilt

- feels without fear

- inhabits their physical form with reverence

The body becomes a temple again — not an obstacle, not a burden, not a machine to be optimized, but a sacred vessel through which presence enters the world.

Embodiment is the bridge between inner awakening and outer action.

The Twelfth Lock: The Fear of Being Seen

The twelfth lock on the Treasure Chest is the **Fear of Being Seen**.

Many people fear visibility because they fear judgment. But the deeper fear is this:

They fear being seen *as they truly are.*

Awakening dissolves this fear.
Not because you become perfect, but because you become honest.

When you no longer hide from yourself, you no longer fear being seen by others.

Presence is transparency.
Transparency is freedom.

Reflection for the Reader: Stop, Look, Listen

Stop: Notice how you enter a room. Do you shrink, perform, or simply arrive?

Look: Observe one interaction today. What would it look like to show up with full presence?

Listen: What part of you is still afraid of being seen? What truth is it protecting?

Chapter 13: The Reclaimed Life

Awakening is not an escape from the world.
It is a return to it — transformed.

The Pilgrimage of the Inner Dawn has brought you through the architecture of the Cage, through the depths of your own interior, and into the rebirth of the heart. Now you stand at the threshold of a new life — not a different life in circumstance, but a different life in consciousness.

This chapter is the integration of everything you have seen, felt, and become.
It is the moment where awakening becomes embodiment.

The Life That Is Truly Yours

Most people live a life that was handed to them — shaped by culture, expectation, fear, and habit. The awakened human begins to live a life that arises from within.

A reclaimed life is not defined by:

- status

- achievement

- image

- productivity

- approval

It is defined by alignment.

Alignment between:

- what you know

- what you feel

- what you value

- what you choose

- what you embody

When these converge, life becomes coherent.
Not easier — but truer.

The End of Fragmentation

Before awakening, the self was divided:

- the public self

- the private self

- the digital self

- the wounded self

- the aspirational self

Each pulling in a different direction.

After awakening, these fragments begin to dissolve.
You no longer need to perform one identity while hiding
another.
You no longer need to curate a persona to be acceptable.
You no longer need to betray your inner truth to survive.

You become one person — whole, integrated, undivided.

This is the quiet miracle of the reclaimed life.

The Sovereignty of Choice

The awakened human does not drift.
They choose.

Not impulsively.
Not reactively.
Not mechanically.

They choose from presence.
They choose from clarity.
They choose from the heart.

Sovereignty is not control over the world.
It is mastery over your inner state.

You cannot dictate what happens to you.
But you can choose how you meet it.
And in that choice, you reclaim your life.

The Courage to Live Truthfully

A reclaimed life is not always comfortable.
Truth rarely is.

To live truthfully means:

- saying no when you mean no

- saying yes when you mean yes

- refusing to betray your conscience

- refusing to shrink Your Soul

- refusing to participate in what fractures you

- refusing to abandon what calls you

Truth is not a philosophy.
It is a posture.

The awakened human stands in truth not because it is easy,
but because it is the only ground that does not collapse
beneath them.

The Human Who Cannot Be Caged

The Cage still exists.
The Influential Few still shape the age.
The world remains noisy, distracted, and fragmented.

But you are no longer the Last Human — the predictable, programmable, compliant creature the age attempted to produce.

You have become something else:

- a human with depth

- a human with presence

- a human with discernment

- a human with a living heart

- a human who sees clearly

- a human who chooses consciously

- a human who cannot be caged

This is the return.
Not to the old life, but to the world as a new being.

The Thirteenth Lock: The Fear of Living Fully

The final lock on the Treasure Chest is the **Fear of Living Fully**.

It is the fear of stepping into your power.
The fear of embodying your truth.
The fear of becoming the person you were always meant to be.

This fear dissolves not through force, but through practice
— the daily choice to live from the awakened heart rather
than the conditioned mind.

Living fully is not a destination.
It is a discipline.

The Treasure Chest Opens

You have identified every lock:

1. The Illusion of Autonomy

2. The Illusion of Indispensability

3. The Confusion of Image with Identity

4. The Loss of Interior Depth

5. The Substitution of Persona for Person

6. The Severing of Body and Being

7. The Fear of Seeing

8. The Fear of the Inner World

9. The Addiction to Elsewhere

10. The Fear of Feeling

11. The Temptation to Retreat

12. The Fear of Being Seen

13. The Fear of Living Fully

And now the Treasure Chest opens.

Inside is not a secret.
Not a doctrine.
Not a technique.

Inside is **you** — the human you were before the world
taught you to forget yourself.

The Pilgrimage is complete.
The Dawn has risen.
The Human has returned.

Reflection for the Reader: Stop, Look, Listen

Stop: Stand still for a moment. Feel the life within you.
Recognize its sacredness.

Look: See the world with new eyes. What calls you
now? What no longer holds you?

Listen: What is the next true step your heart is asking
you to take?

EPILOGUE: THE DAWN BEYOND THE PAGE

The journey you have taken through these pages is not the end.

It is the beginning.

You have seen the Cage.
You have walked through the night.
You have felt the stirring of the heart and the return of presence.
You have stood at the threshold of a reclaimed life.

But awakening is not a single moment.
It is a rhythm — a continual turning toward what is true.

The world you return to is the same world you left at the beginning of this book:
noisy, distracted, fragmented, and shaped by forces that do not honor the depth of the human soul.

But *you* are no longer the same.

You carry within you:

- a new clarity

- a new stillness

- a new courage

- a new way of seeing

- a new way of being

The Pilgrimage of the Inner Dawn is not a path you walk once.

It is a path you walk daily — in your choices, your
presence, your attention, your compassion, your truth.

The Cage may remain, but you are no longer its inhabitant.
You are its witness.
You are its challenger.
You are its transcendence.

The world does not need more noise.
It does not need more speed.
It does not need more performance.

It needs humans — real humans —
humans with depth, with heart, with presence, with
integrity, with courage.

Humans who remember who they are.

If you carry even a spark of this remembrance into your
life, the Dawn will continue to rise — not only within you,
but around you.

The Pilgrimage is yours now.
Walk it with sincerity.
Walk it with courage.
Walk it with an awakened heart.

The Dawn is already within you.

Let it shine.

ACKNOWLEDGMENTS

No book is born from a single mind.
Every page carries the imprint of countless lives,
encounters, and moments of grace that shaped the author
long before a single word was written.

To those who walked beside me in silence —
who offered presence rather than instruction,
who listened without trying to fix,
who believed in the possibility of renewal even when I
could not see it —
your quiet strength lives in these pages.

To the thinkers, poets, mystics, and rebels whose voices
echoed across centuries and stirred my own awakening —
your courage to speak truth in dark times lit the path I now
walk.
This work stands on the foundation you laid.

To the few who challenged me, confronted me, and
refused to let me settle for half-truths —
your honesty sharpened my discernment and deepened my
resolve.
You reminded me that love and truth are inseparable.

To those who have suffered under the weight of a world
that has forgotten the human soul —
your longing for meaning, dignity, and inner freedom is the
heartbeat of this book.
You are not alone.
Your struggle is seen.
Your awakening matters.

And finally, to the reader —
thank you for your courage to turn inward,

to question the age,
to reclaim your presence,
and to walk the Pilgrimage of the Inner Dawn with
sincerity.
This book is no longer mine.
It belongs to you now,
to your journey,
to your becoming.

May the Dawn you carry illuminate the world you touch.

READER'S GUIDE

The works in this Canon are not a series of books.
They are a sequence of thresholds —
each one revealing a deeper layer of orientation,
each one restoring the human being to the Real.

Every volume stands alone,
yet each one prepares the reader for the next.
Together, they form a single philosophical architecture:
the journey from collapse to clarity,
from illusion to awakening,
from disorientation to the return of the Real.

Below is the map of that journey.

THE CANON

1. GOD CANNOT DIE

The Collapse of Human Orientation, Not the Collapse of the Divine
The entry point.
This book diagnoses the fracture of the modern mind,
exposes the illusion that the eternal can collapse,
and guides the reader back to sanity.

It restores orientation
and prepares the reader for the thresholds ahead.

2. THE BURDEN OF COMFORT

How Comfort Becomes Captivity
This volume reveals how comfort becomes a prison,
how the familiar becomes a trap,
and how the human being slowly loses itself
in the pursuit of ease.

It is the first confrontation with the self
and the beginning of the awakening.

3. THE BOOK OF THRESHOLDS

Crossings That Change a Life
A ceremonial map of the inner thresholds
every human must cross to awaken.

Each threshold is a rupture,
a moment of truth,
a point of no return.

This book is the architecture of transformation.

4. THE LAST HUMAN

The Collapse of the False Self
This volume explores what remains
when every illusion, identity, and false foundation
collapses.

It is the stripping away of the old self
and the moment the human stands alone
before the Real.

5. THE PILGRIM OF THE INNER DAWN

(Trilogy)
The journey inward.
The long walk through shadow, memory, and meaning
toward the first light of awakening.

This trilogy reveals the inner landscape
the human must traverse
to reach the dawn within.

6. THE PURSUIT OF TRUTH

(Trilogy)
The outward journey.
The search for the Real beyond the self —
the quest for the One who grounds all things.

This trilogy confronts the limits of human thought,
the hunger for meaning,
and the encounter with the eternal.

7. GOD BEYOND EXISTENCE

The Being Who Cannot Be Contained
This volume reveals the truth
that the One we seek
is not an object within reality
but the ground of reality itself.

It is the culmination of the metaphysical arc
and the beginning of a new understanding of the divine.

8. The Journey Continues – *TBA*

The final volume —
not an ending,
but an opening.

This book explores what it means
to live from the new orientation,
to walk in clarity,
to embody sanity,
and to continue the journey
with the Real beneath every step.

How to Read the Canon

The Canon is not meant to be rushed.
It is meant to be lived.

Readers may:

- pause between volumes

- reread thresholds that resonate

- sit with the questions that arise

- allow the architecture to unfold in its own time

Each book is a crossing.
Each crossing is a return.

A Final Word to the Reader

If you have reached this point,
you have already crossed the first threshold.

The Canon continues from here —
not to overwhelm you,
but to guide you deeper
into the clarity that has already begun.

Welcome to the path.

GLOSSARY OF KEY CONCEPTS

This glossary is not a dictionary of technical terms.
It is a guide to the symbolic language of *The Last Human* —
the metaphors, archetypes, and inner realities that shape
the Pilgrimage of the Inner Dawn.
Use it as a companion as you revisit the journey.

The Cage

The invisible structure of modern conditioning —
psychological, technological, economic, and cultural — that
shapes human behavior without requiring force.
The Cage is not a place but a pattern: a way of living that
numbs depth, fragments attention, and replaces
authenticity with performance.

The Influential Few

The small group of technocratic, economic, and cultural
architects who design the systems that guide modern
desire, attention, and identity.
They are not villains but engineers of a world optimized for
efficiency rather than humanity.

The Last Human

The modern individual shaped by the Cage — predictable,
distracted, fragmented, and increasingly disconnected from
inner life, embodiment, and truth.
The Last Human is not a person but a condition.

The New Human

The awakened individual who has reclaimed presence,
discernment, depth, and inner sovereignty.
The New Human is not a perfected being but a person
who lives consciously and refuses to be shaped by the age.

The Locks

Thirteen psychological and spiritual barriers that prevent
awakening.
Each lock represents a form of fear, illusion, or
conditioning that keeps the Treasure Chest closed.
The Pilgrimage involves recognizing and dissolving these
locks one by one.

The Treasure Chest

The symbolic container of the true self — the
unfragmented, unconditioned, authentic human essence
buried beneath layers of habit, fear, and cultural
programming.
Opening the Treasure Chest is the culmination of the
Pilgrimage.

The Pilgrimage of the Inner Dawn

The inner journey from unconscious living to awakened
presence.
It is not a physical path but a transformation of perception,
attention, and heart.
The Pilgrimage unfolds in three movements: seeing the
Cage, awakening the heart, and returning to the world
transformed.

Presence

The state of being fully here — attentive, embodied, and
aware.
Presence is the antidote to distraction and the foundation
of awakening.
It is not a technique but a way of inhabiting reality.

Discernment

The inner capacity to distinguish truth from illusion, depth from noise, and authenticity from performance.
Discernment arises naturally when the mind becomes quiet and the heart becomes clear.

The Inner Witness

The quiet, observing awareness within you that sees without judgment and recognizes truth before it is understood.
The Witness is the first sign of awakening and the guide throughout the Pilgrimage.

The Heart

The center of meaning, conscience, intuition, and love.
Not merely emotional, the heart is the organ of spiritual perception.
Its rebirth marks the turning point of the Pilgrimage.

Embodiment

The return to the physical self — living through the senses, honoring the body, and grounding awareness in the present moment.
Embodiment reconnects the awakened human to reality.

The Return

The final movement of the Pilgrimage, where the awakened individual re-enters the world with clarity, presence, and inner sovereignty.
The Return is not withdrawal but participation from a deeper state of being.

The Dawn

The symbolic light of awakening — the inner illumination that arises when the heart, mind, and body come into alignment.

The Dawn is not an event but a continual unfolding.

ABOUT THE AUTHOR

Conde D. Cagalitan is a philosopher, writer, and contemplative whose work explores the inner architecture of human awakening in an age of distraction, fragmentation, and spiritual amnesia. His writing is rooted in a lifelong inquiry into truth — not as an abstract concept, but as a lived reality that shapes the human heart and restores the dignity of the soul.

Drawing from classical realism, metaphysics, and the perennial wisdom traditions, The author work seeks to illuminate the path from unconscious living to conscious presence. He writes for those who sense that something essential has been lost in the modern world — and who feel called to rediscover the depth, clarity, and inner sovereignty that lie beneath the noise.

His approach is both rigorous and compassionate: a blend of philosophical precision, poetic resonance, and practical guidance. He believes that personal transformation is the foundation of collective renewal, and that every human being carries within them a spark of dawn waiting to be awakened.

The Last Human is the second volume in a larger body of work dedicated to the journey of inner rebirth and the restoration of meaning in a disoriented age. Cagalitan continues to write, teach, and guide others on the Pilgrimage of the Inner Dawn — the path toward becoming fully, consciously, and courageously human.

www.ingramcontent.com/pod-product-compliance
Lightning Source LLC
Chambersburg PA
CBHW051816050726
47598CB00006B/2585